Accent Reduction For Professionals

How to eliminate your accent to sound more American

Whitney Nelson

Table of Contents

Bonus

Introduction

It may frustrate you endlessly – especially as a professional with goals of being successful in your career. The fact that many find your accent "charming" doesn't compensate much. It certainly doesn't mean it'll make you successful.

Of course, your accent is less than charming when it prevents someone from understanding what you're saying. It's less than charming when you find yourself repeating yourself. It's especially frustrating and less than charming when you discover that your accent is actually preventing you from advancing in your chosen career.

While this book is useful to all individuals who wish to reduce their accent and sound more like a native speaker, it's written with the professional individual in mind. If your English language skills are solid, your grasp of the vocabulary solid and you're comfortable speaking the language itself, then you may very well be searching for the last piece of the puzzle. Eliminating the accent so you can not only be understood a bit more easily, but feel like you're a better fit into your office environment.

As sad as it may seem, a strong accent when speaking English can actually keep you from achieving your career goals as well as reaching your full potential. It has been proven that when some individuals continually ask you to repeat yourself, it can lower your chances of professional advancement. In other words, enunciating your words and using correct grammar are two requirements to conquer the business world today.

I know how serious you are about your career. Because of this, I also know how serious you are about improving both your pronunciation and in the process reducing and eliminating your accent. This book deals specifically with helping you speak more like a native.

Working with Your Accent

Before you get the wrong idea, there's absolutely nothing "wrong" with a foreign accent. Everyone – even native speakers of English – have some type of accent. Have you ever traveled to Boston or New York and listened in on conversations residents of those cities hold on the street?

Arguably, there are also situations when you can use your accent to your advantage. If you want move from being considered at "very good" at the English language to the next level, "excellent," then you need to make a concerted effort to help soften your accent.

We'll help you do just that. Once you've conquered your accent, you'll notice how confident you are in talking not only to your supervisors, colleagues and clients, but also at making presentations.

What is an Accent?

In the largest sense of the word, an accent is how you sound when you speak. Generally speaking, there are two types of accents. The first is what is most commonly identified as a "foreign" accent. This accent is the natural lingering effects of learning, let's say English, using (consciously or unconsciously) the rules or sounds of your native language.

It's actually a coping mechanism, if you really think about it. When you're learning English as a second language, you may encounter some difficulty making all of the sounds of English. There are several sounds that no other language contains. Or it could be that your mouth isn't cooperating because it never had to say these sounds before.

The accent occurs when you substitute similar sounds, drawn from your native language. It's called a "foreign" accent simply because it sounds "foreign" to those who are native speakers of English.

The second type of accent, which we lightly touched on earlier, is the one which is used by a specific group of native speakers, usually clustered in a general geographical location. These individuals have cultivated certain pronunciations that are unique to them. Consider the classic Boston accent. Or the accent you'll find among many in New York City. If you travel the United States at all, you'll discover variations of accents. From North Carolina, to Kentucky to Texas, each of these areas contain their own accents.

Why are some Sounds Difficult for Some Individuals?

Some people, you'll notice, have a difficult time with sounds that are new to them. The truth is, if you would have learned these sounds when you were an infant, you wouldn't have any trouble at all with them. Children are born with the amazing ability of being able to pronounce all the sounds of every language.

As an infant matures, however, she or he soon learns which specific sounds are important in his language. He then simply ignores the others. If the sounds don't serve the infant and he doesn't use them, you can see how easily it could be for that ability to slip away.

Linguists say that by the time children reach one year of age, they've intuitively learned which sounds don't serve them and simply disregard them. As we age then, these sounds become increasingly more difficult to pronounce.

Individual sounds aren't the only reason you may find yourself speaking with an accent. There are elements to any language called "sound patterns." Specific sound patterns naturally differ among languages. To fully understand this you'll need to look an example or two.

A syllable in an English word may begin or end with a cluster of consonants, like "str" and "ngth." Right now, think of the word strength. This word contains both of those. This is different than the Japanese language, in which a typical syllable contains no more than one consonant immediately followed by one vowel. The examples here are in "ma" or "ki."

For native Japanese speakers, pronouncing these consonant clusters can be problematic. This is why they may place a vowel sound between the consonants in an English cluster.

Another cause of a foreign accent may be derived from the natural sentence structuring of the language. This problem often crops up in Russian. An excellent example is found in the English sentence "The house is very large." The problem for the native speaking Russian is that there is no word corresponding to the English word "the." Therefore, he doesn't see it as essential to speaking it in English.

The second problem is that Russian doesn't require the speaker to place the verb "is" in the sentence. So, if you're translating the sentence into English, the typical Russian speaker would be inclined to simply say, "House very large." While it sounds perfect to the Russian ear, it sounds clumsy to the English ear.

Is Eliminating Accent Really Necessary?

Many students of English ask if eliminating their accent is really necessary. For some, it may not be. There are many individuals who take great pride in their accent. My grandmother, whose first language was Slovak never lost her accent. I suspect that she retained it out of a sense of pride. That doesn't mean she didn't have a great grasp of English. She did. She lived to be 87 years old and always talked with an accent. But then, she was essential a farmer and a stay-at-home mom.

Examine your career honestly and you'll probably come to the conclusion that it would help you immensely. If you find yourself having difficulty communicating with others due to the way you speak the English language, you may consider reducing it. Just what are the "difficulties" you may experiencing? A very few of these are listed below:

People not understanding you.

I can't tell you how many of my friends and family refuse to go to an excellent doctor or other medical specialist because they have difficulty understanding their strong accent. I can't help but think it's a shame to not avail themselves on what could possibly be the best possible health care they may get.

In many college settings, students give up or refuse to take certain courses because the instructor or professor speaks with a foreign accent. As with the health profession, a student may be passing up the chance to experience a great course.

Avoiding social interaction with those who may not understand you.

In these instances, you're missing out on what may be the best areas of your life, getting together with good friends. Why cut yourself off from social interactions needlessly?

Frustration from having to repeat yourself all the time.

Many individuals find it frustrating to have to continually repeat themselves because they can't be understood. You may not only be frustrated when you speak, you may also hesitate to speak. Why not enjoy all the aspects of a good conversation and the interactions of good friends?

People focusing on your accent more than on what you are trying to say.

We mentioned this problem at the opening of the introduction. There are some individuals who'll find your accent "charming" and get lost in the melodious sounds and ignore the message. If this happens to you, think about reducing your accent. You'll find they're less likely to comment on your accent and more wiling to talk about the substance of what you said.

When Problems Turn Into Barriers

But these problems with communication go deeper than what I've outline above. When the problems are severe enough and occur frequently, these seemingly minor problems can avalanche into barriers in any number of ways. They could hinder your job performance, your advancement in college as well as making your personal life less than satisfying.

So many individuals also tell me their accent is lowering their self-esteem. It's easy to see why. Having to repeat yourself, trying to get your point across and just thinking twice before saying anything in public is sure to have some effect on how you view yourself.

Before you begin to think that it's impossible to eliminate your foreign accent, I'm here to tell you that it's not only possible, but probably easier than what you believe it to be. With even a little concentration and practice you'll find yourself speaking like a native in no time at all.

The key words, though, are concentration and practice. It's not something that's going to happen overnight. Then, again, you probably already know this because you didn't learn how to speak English overnight.

Right now you're so close to mastering the language it would be a shame if you didn't take that extra step to eliminate that accent.

What's In This Book to Help You?

This book is divided into ten chapters, starting explaining why a strong accents can reduce your chances of getting hired. It's difficult to have any type of career if you can't get past the first hurdle getting hired.

From there, I take you through the most important steps you'll need to take in order to speak more like a native. Together, we'll be reviewing the various sounds that usually trick and trip those who have learned English as a second language, such as the vowel sounds – a, e, i, and u – as well as what syllables to stress with certain words.

In addition, you'll learn what the soft palate is and why it's important in reducing your accent. This book will provide you with examples and exercises you can use to help in this area.

There are certain letters and sounds in English that can even challenge native speakers. Take the "r" sound for example. Native Japanese speakers naturally find this sound difficult.

But you'd be amazed at how many individuals who have learned English as their native language also stumble on this.

I should know. As a grade-school student I went to speech therapy to learn the proper way to pronounce the letter "r." To this day, I find myself occasionally, not pronouncing it properly, especially if I'm tired.

Sounds like the "th" may be difficult for you to say, which may, in turn, contribute to your accent. There are few, if any, other languages that even have this sound. So, it's naturally a problem for many people who are learning English as a second language.

But that's not all you'll learn in this small book. We'll review intonation, which is nothing more than the natural melody, flow and pitch of a language, the use of diphthongs (two letters strung together to make one sound) which aren't found in all other languages.

You'll also discover how to put all these disparate segments of the English language together. You'll discover in the last two chapters of this volume, not only how to combine all this learning, but the best methods of practicing them.

It may sound overwhelming at the moment, but as you tackle each of these areas one by one, you'll notice how your accent softens and with time, patience and practice actually disappears.

Are you ready to start your next step in learning the English language – that of reducing and eventually eliminating your accent?

Then, let's get started.

Chapter 1: Is Your Strong Accent Preventing you from Getting your Perfect Job?

It's not fair, you might say. You'd be right. Nonetheless, it occurs every day.

Imagine this scenario. Two individuals interview for the same position with a corporation. Both are equally qualified. One speaks English like a native. The other person speaks with a foreign accent. Who gets the job?

If you said the native speaker, then you already know the odds are swinging that way. Everyone knows that potential employers can't discriminate in the hiring process based on race or gender. But what if an individual were denied a position because of the accent associated with his speech? Could an employer not hire and individual based on the way he speaks the English language?

Legally speaking, I'm not sure that issue has ever been tested in court, but that is probably something that happens more often than most of us would ever suspect. Perhaps it has even happened to you. Have you ever felt you were excluded from the short list of candidates or actually not hired because of your speech and speech patterns?

If you have been the victim of this type of hiring practice, then you've no doubt walked out of the office depressed and angry, to name but a few emotions. You know you have to keep looking, but your chest tightens just thinking about going through the interview ordeal and hiring process again.

That being said, you've got to be realistic about your accent as well. Some positions require public speaking. Some even require speaking with no identifiable accent. For example, listen to all the national news correspondents. What type of accent do you hear?

None. Normally a news reporter doesn't even have an American regional accent. Many of the native English speakers take elocution lessons to learn how to speak without an accent. Consider the actor who plays the lead in the now-defunct television series, House. What kind of accent does he speak with? If you can't detect an identifiable accent, you're right.

But have you ever heard him on national talk shows? He speaks with a definitive English accent. Which is natural, since he was born in Oxford, English. He's only one of many actors and actresses who can slip in and out of accents seemingly with ease.

Granted, you may not hunger to be an actor and news reporting may not be your profession. Consider the typical business positions, though. Many of these require you to stand up and speak to a group of potential investors or clients or even your colleagues. As with the individual you initially hired you, they're trying not to prejudge you based solely on your accent.

If your accent is so thick that you're spending more time repeating and explaining yourself than concentrating on your method that doesn't forebode well. At this point, your thoughts may be turning negative. "Will I ever find a job at this rate?" you're asking yourself.

You've heard the saying before. "If you keep doing what you've always been doing, you're always going to get what you've always got."

Not eloquent. But true. So how does this pertain to you? Perhaps it's time to take the first steps to change that accent?

No, it won't be easy, even linguists admit this. Listen to what Dianne Markley, a professor at the University of North Texas at Denton, says about learning a second language later in life, like you did.

"It's nearly impossible to speak any acquired later in life without an accent." The kicker in this scenario is the research she's unearthed in her academic research. There exists "an incredibly strong statistical correlation between judging someone as cultured, intelligent, and competent and placing them into prestigious jobs" based on the *lack of an accent.*

Many Americans are guilty of this when it comes to their fellow countrymen. While it's not very popular to admit of late, you'd be astonished to discover what some northerners think of those who speak with a dialect normally associated with the south, especially with West Virginia and Kentucky. Or perhaps you wouldn't.

Not Really a Conspiracy

Some people may view this as an intentional conspiracy or some subversive racist behavior. But Victor Arias, who is a manager partner a Heidrick and Struggles said that really isn't the case. He's involved in diversity practices for the executive search firm.

Instead, accents tend to trigger emotions in a subtle way. These emotions, he said, "may make a difference." It's clear he admits that "people "make judgments based on accents."

This doesn't mean this near-instant judgments are all negative, Arias added. But, this is where the idea of discrimination may appear. "Not only may someone with a Hispanic accent may be perceived as less educated," he said. "An individual with a British accent may be seen as "more intelligent." This occurs daily, despite the fact there's absolutely nothing to base this judgment on except the opinion of the person listening.

But that's only the tip of the iceberg. What if someone was interviewed for a job who spoke with an Asian accent? How would that affect his or her chances of winning the position?

Marley explains an Asian accept could be the edge that candidate needed if he or she were interviewing at a scientific or engineering firm. She concluded that these issues aren't set in stone. "They're all very situational."

Even the intensity of the accent triggers certain feelings. Arias readily admits that someone with only a slight accent may be seen by many "as more educated or worldly than someone with a thick accent."

He continues. "I've fallen for that," he said. He has heard both the thick and thin accent and made a rash judgment. He concluded the person's level of education based on hearing him talk and later admonished himself for jumping to that conclusion.

Before we go any further, let's get one thing straight. An accent is nothing more than a pattern of pronunciation. It's in no way a reflection of how well the person uses language. He may speak with a thick accent and speak impeccable English. Despite this, to the native speaker's ear, he may be perceived as an individual who cannot adequately fill the position for which he's applying.

No one is defending this behavior, especially those in charge of doing the hiring. Indeed, candidate – all candidates – should be chosen on their qualifications and only that. But that's not always the case.

Do you recall earlier in this chapter we asked if denying a person a position based on his accent were legal? Apparently it is. Marley uses the position of a customer service representative as a prime example. One of the prime requirements for this position, she explains, is that the candidate has excellent communication skills. An individual who could not be well understood over the phone could very well disrupt the flow of business.

Again, though, this is only the tip of the iceberg, Markley explains. When an employer denies a candidate the position as an excuse to discriminate against his national original, then that's definitely illegal. Take the case of two candidates for the same position. One candidate has a thick Hispanic accent; the other possesses an equally thick French accent.

An employer can't choose the candidate with the French accent over the other based solely on his pattern of speech. That, in effect, would be discrimination.

As you can see, that when you interview for a job, regardless of how qualified you may be, you may be at the mercy of the person doing the hiring more so than an individual who speaks English as his first language.

Once again, we repeat. No one said that was fair. In fairness to those who do to the hiring, for the most part, these persons try hard to ignore these aspects. There's also much on the line for them as well. There's a lesson to be learned here for the person doing the hiring. He needs to be aware of the possibility of an unintended and certainly unconscious bias against those who speak with foreign accents.

But there are definitely lessons for those who speak with the accent to learn. Believe it or not, an accent does serve a purpose. One of the most important things it does is connect you and your family with a specific part of the world. In short, it's part of your heritage. Viewed from this perspective, an accent is not a negative thing.

Going for the Interview

Why, of course, you need to interview for your dream job despite your accent. You can't just wring your hands and complain, "Poor me!" You've already got enough stress working when you're job searching. When you do step into that office for the interview and the door closes behind you, keep these few simple rules in mind.

First, use your best grammar. That alone will set you apart from many of the candidates. Don't worry, your use of proper grammar practices will be heard above your accent, regardless of how strong you believe it is.

The second rule is to speak slowly. This allows your interviewer to process your words easier. Not only that, but it forces you to pay attention to your pronunciation. In many ways, you and the interviewer can reach a happy medium.

Whatever else you do, don't get frustrated if you're asked to repeat yourself. It's not the end of the world. How you handle your language and accent under pressure like that has the potential to impress your potential employer. He or she may decide that based solely on your ability to remain calm under stress, you're just the person they're searching for.

But the best advice of all, comes from Carlos Soto, who in his capacity as president of the National Hispanic Corporate

Council adds this piece of advice as well. "Prepare." Prepare more than any other candidate.

Part of that preparation, he says is to practice your potential answers in English.

Of course, your accent shouldn't make a difference in the hiring process. Unfortunately it does. That means you should do everything within your power to stack the odds in your favor.

In the next chapter, I suggest that the best starting place to speak more like a native is to understand and concentrate on changing where you put stress or emphasis in your words and sentences. This one step will help you in ways you couldn't even imagine right now.

Chapter 2: Can you Hear That? Placing Stress on the Proper Syllables

It seems like such a subtle aspect – the syllables that Americans stress when speaking. Who would believe that this small point can distinguish a native speaker from one who isn't?

The fact is when you already have to learn the meanings of the words swirling around you and sentence structure and the crazy and not extremely constant rules of English grammar, you're already feeling overwhelmed. Worrying about which syllables to stress when speaking out loud is probably the last thing you're concerned about.

Now, though, you're a more advanced English speaker, so advanced that you're using the English language in many different settings. One of these setting is in your workplace. You now can take a breather because you're fluent in the language.

Your focus is on advancing in your career but, you realize that the biggest roadblock you're encountering is your "foreign accent." It's time to start learning what you can do to reduce that accent.

Your first step is to listen to native speakers with an ear toward which syllable is stressed when words contain more than one syllable. Though I'm a native speaker of English, I noticed the differences in this area when I talked with foreign students who learned British English overseas. I'll never forget the first word I heard from an instructor with an accent. The word was "distribute." As a native speaker I've naturally stressed the second syllable. This instructor though stressed the last syllable. This one subtle difference spoke volumes to me.

For some people reducing their accent this could easily mean just changing the syllable stressing of many of the words you're using. If you could do this – and only this -- you may be taking a large stride toward eliminating your accent.

It's not Always the First

Probably the biggest mistake those who learn English as a second language make is assuming that Americans naturally – and always – place the spoken emphasis of a two-syllable word on the first syllable. That just isn't so.

Granted, the stressed first syllable occurs quite a bit in the English language, but it just doesn't show up in every single word.

Speak the following list of words out loud. Listen to yourself closely as you say them.

- Window
- Target

- Baby

- Auto

If you've said them as most Americans do, then the first syllable is emphasized. Take just a moment now and say them again, this time ensuring you're placing the stress on the first syllable of each word.

If you have a really good ear, you'll also hear that when you stress the first syllable the pitch of your voice lowers even while you're still speaking it. If you're near a friend you feel comfortable with right now, ask him or her to say these words while you listen attentively. You may even ask him to listen to you while you say these words. Get his feedback.

If you're having a difficult time conquering this, don't worry. In nearly every other language in the world, the stressed syllable is normally pronounced with a rise in pitch. With enough attention to detail and enough practice, you'll soon be able to do this.

Words with Three or more Syllables

The other mistaken assumption many non-native English speakers make is assuming that all words are spoken emphasizing the first syllable. Nothing could be further from the truth.

Speak these words while emphasizing the underlined syllable

- In tro _duce_

- Dis ap _point_

- En ter _tain_

I wish I can provide you with a quick and easy rule of thumb that makes it easy to recognize which multi-syllabic words are pronounced with a distinct stress pattern. Unfortunately, there are no rules. So it's a matter of listening, learning and repeating. Here again, the more you listen and repeat the words, the easier and more natural you'll become when speaking.

Noun versus Verb: Oh, the Stress!

That's all well and good you say. You can concentrate on that. But you also need to know that the syllable being emphasized depends, believe it or not, whether the word is being used as a noun or a verb within the sentence. In essence, how you pronounce the word is dependent on the context in which it's being used. Emphasizing the wrong syllable here also reveals your accent.

You've probably encountered more than your fair share of words that are used as both nouns and verbs. These words are spelled the same, but when used as a noun the stress falls on one syllable. When used as a verb, a different syllable should be stressed. This is more than just a lesson in semantics. Placing the emphasis on the wrong syllable depending on its use actually gives the word an entirely different meaning.

As a rule of thumb, when the first syllable is emphasized you can be fairly confident the word is being used as a noun. If you detect the second syllable is emphasized then you can be relatively sure the word is being used as a verb. If you place the emphasis on the "wrong" syllable, then you may very well be changing the entire meaning of the word without knowing it. Listen to yourself closely as you say the following two sentences out loud. Better yet, if you have a native-English speaking friend recite these out loud. Listen to see if you can tell on which syllable the emphasis is placed.

Your *conduct* was outrageous.

Rick and Jane will *conduct* the meeting.

In the first sentence, the initial syllable of the word conduct is emphasized. In the second example the second syllable is stressed. Is there really a difference in meaning between the two pronunciations?

Indeed, there is. The noun means how a person acts. The verb means to take charge of or to direct a group of individuals. If you emphasize the wrong syllable of the word when you use it in a sentence, you may not only confuse yourself, but others as well. The following words are those that also fall into this category – two different ways of pronouncing the same word which gives that word two separate meanings.

- Contract
- Suspect

- Insert

- Subject

- Insert

Looking Within: the Sentence that is!

There's yet another way to reduce your accent and sound more like a native speaker. That's by knowing which words to stress within the sentence itself. Again, this is not just some silly rule, even though you may think so. The words you choose to emphasis in a sentence has the potential to change the meaning of the sentence.

When spoken, the English language indicates stress by pronouncing a word or a phrase either slightly louder or longer (or sometimes both). You may also be able to indicate emphasis within a sentence by changing your pitch of certain words.

You need to realize, though, that we aren't talking about altering the stress of the syllables of the words. This requires simply changing the stress of the words in the sentence.

The following is a single sentence to give you an example of how changing the emphasis of one of the words in the sentence can give it a different connotation. Let's use the following sentence as an example.

Rose bought a gorgeous outfit.

When you say this sentence with the word Rose emphasized, **Rose** bought a gorgeous outfit, you're defining who did the buying. It was Rose, not Mary or Jan.

Rose **bought** a gorgeous outfit.

When you place the emphasis on the word bought, you're making sure your listeners know that Rose purchased the dress, it was not given to her (or she stole it!).

If you've really never thought of this before, you may be a bit puzzled now. While there are many rules in the English language and many exceptions as well, there is one dealing with the emphasis of words within sentences that you can usually follow with confidence.

For the most part, native speakers tend to emphasize content words, not the function words. Content words are readily recognizable: nouns, verbs, adjectives and adverbs. On the other hand, function words are those that are consider parts of speech articles, prepositions and conjunctions. The second category of words isn't usually emphasized since they're considered transition words.

As transition words, they don't carry the vital information the content words do.

Another way of emphasizing your speech which will help reduce your accent is studying the category of words known as compound words. This is a word created by placing two words with separate meanings together to form one word with a more specific meaning. Think of the word "bathtub."

In English the word bath is a noun with a meaning of its own and the word "tub" has a meaning and can be used in many situations. When you place these two words together, you get a specific meaning.

So which word do you stress within that compound word? Again, for the most part the first word of that compound word is emphasized. Below are just several compound words in which the first word is stressed. Read the list below out loud. Be sure to emphasize the first word when you read these:

- Thunderstorm
- Birthday
- Cupcake
- Toothbrush
- Earthquake

The sooner you start putting these rules on emphasis and stress into action, the sooner you'll be on the road to reducing that accent.

Do you know what that means? The sooner you're on the road to opening new and exciting doors in your career. Knowing which syllables to emphasis when speaking is only part of the knowledge needed (and to be implemented). There are still a few hints that can carry you even farther in your quest to reduce your accent. The next section introduces you to these.

Syllables: Still More Secrets to Reveal

Shh! There are still two more secrets native English speakers know that you may not be aware of regarding proper emphasis on words. If you're not aware of these "secrets" you may find you'll never be spot on when it comes to sounding like a native.

Don't get upset. These native speakers aren't deliberating keeping these secrets from you. The truth is that they probably don't even know they exist. I venture to go one step further and claim they probably don't even know what they're doing. They couldn't reveal these secrets even if they wanted to.

We'll talk first about the "ing" sound you see at the end of many English words. When a word ends with a combination of these letters, it's safe to say the emphasis is not on the last syllable. For example, say the word "trying." You'll notice that only the first syllable is stressed. If you can't hear it when you speak it, ask someone else to say this word out loud and listen to it carefully.

Here's a word with even more syllable that follow this rule: demonstrating. Native English speakers only stress the first syllable. You'll find a similar pattern in the word *negotiating*. Only in this word, you'll stress the second syllable, the "go" sound.

This is a rule you can take to the bank. The only exception, of course, (Let's face it, this is English. You'd be disappointed if there weren't any exceptions.) refers to single-syllable words ending in the "ing" sound, like "sing," "fling," or "sting."

When Words End in "ion"

Here's another fairly solid rule of pronunciation. It's based in the "ion" that you've no doubt have come across. You can be sure that the stressed syllable isn't the "ion" ending, rather it's on the syllable directly before it. Even in pronouncing seemingly smaller words the rule still holds up. It works for the word, union, for example as well as the two-syllable word million.

Let's look at the word negotiation. Even though the "ion" sound is pronounced differently (like "shun"), you're still not emphasizing the "ion" sound. You are, however, stressing two other syllables in negotiation.

The next step in your accent reduction program is to learning how native speakers use the vowel sounds: a, e, i, o, and u. Follow me to the next chapter to discover how.

Chapter 3: Learning the Sounds of the Vowels

A, E, I, O, U.

This chapter explains in simple language how to properly pronounce the vowels in order to reduce your accent.

One of the very first aspects of the English language you learned, no doubt, was the differences in sounds between the consonants and vowels. The vowels, of course, are a, e, i, o, and u. How you develop the pronunciation of these five letters will determine your ability to speak like a native.

It would be great if I could tell you that those five vowels contain only five separate and distinct sounds. The truth is though, as you're well aware of, that's just not the truth. There's not only several pronunciations of each of those five vowels, but depending on what syllable you stress in a word, you'll discover yet one more variation of how to pronounce it.

If it sounds messy . . . well, it is. But at the same time, messy isn't quite the same thing as hard. And messy doesn't mean it's not worth tidying the mess up a bit and buckling down and learning and practicing the difference in the spoken word – especially when it's instrumental in losing your accent.

If you recall, we've already talked about how the stressed sounds of English are pronounced. Unlike many languages, those words or syllables that are stressed are, for the most part descend in pitch. You only have to pronounced the vowels to get a good idea of what I mean. Why not say them out loud (You're exempt from this suggestion if you're in a library or other quiet area. Then that suggestion is problematic.)

- A
- E
- I
- O
- U

As you say these out loud, listen closely to how each of these actually do descend in pitch. You could also ask a native speaker, whom you trust to say them out loud. Listen closely to see if you can detect a difference in your pronunciation from his. This might be a part of your accent reduction program that you may need to hone to perfection.

As part of this process, you should also study some of the following sentences we've created to serve as examples and training your pronunciation of the spoken word. Keep in mind that all of the emphasized the sounds you voice should naturally be lowered in pitch. I've italicized the words which need emphasized and the pitch lowered.

Let's Start with A

Since it's the first letter of the alphabet it seems the logical place to start. The first thing you should know about this sound is that it actually takes two steps in order to pronounce it accurately.

You begin by pushing your tongue forward in the mouth and then as you're closing your jaw, you move the body of your tong upward until it almost reaches the tooth ridge. At the same time the sides of the tongue touch the top teeth as you finish enunciating the sound.

Here are a few sentences to get you started.

His secret is *safe* with me.

You, madam, are no *lady*.

Don't you dare *take* advantage of me!

You'll probably need a *safety* net if you insist on doing that.

This marks a big *change* for me.

Maybe she should *make* more cookies?

The pie crust needs to be *flaky*.

Maybe I should *name* the actress' *age*.

EEK!: Listening to the Long E Sound

When you're pronouncing the English long "e" sound properly, you'll immediately notice the sound actually resonates slightly off your lower teeth, as a bright, sharp sound.

In order to pronounce this sound correctly, your tongue should be positioned toward the front of your mouth. In fact, the body of the tongue should be close to the tooth ridge. Ensure that the tongue is higher in the mouth than for the other vowel sounds. You'll notice that this tongue position nearly automatically closes the jaw. The sides of your tongue should touch the top side teeth while you're enunciating this vowel.

You can practice making this sound by repeating out loud any or all of the following sentences. The italicized words should be pronounced as a long "e" sound.

Keep the *keys.*

I don't *need* to *read* it.

They are *meeting* by the oak *tree.*

It's human nature to thirst for *freedom.*

She was *relieved* to *clean* the mess.

If you believe you're struggling with this sound, then ask a trusted friend to read these sentences out loud to you. You can pantomime the words while she's enunciating them or repeat them after her – or both.

In order to make the most progress, you may want to work in a "safe" environment – with a friend who's only concerned with your ultimate progress.

Listen to the Long I Sound

What exactly are you listening for? Technically, this sound is composed of two separate sounds that ends with a brief "y" sound. The first step in pronouncing this vowel is to place the tongue within the mouth so it touches the bottom side teeth.

Once you've learned that, then you close the jaw slightly, while the body of the tongue moves upward until it nearly touches the tooth ridge. Again, this position should remind you of the position of the "y" sound. The sides of the tongue, near the front, actually should touch inside of the top, side teeth.

You can hear the long "I" clearly in the following words: guy, invite, sign surprise, while, why. Here are some sentences below you can repeat saying as examples:

She's *trying* to do what is *right.*

Good *night,* sweet prince!

My mother never *liked* that *kind* of talk.

He's a *fine* man.

Look for a new *kind* of *society* to emerge.

Notice that some of these sentences contain more than one long "i" sound. You must pronounce each sound the same way. This is a sure method to temper your accent and sound more like a native speaker.

As you begin practicing you'll probably need to consciously make an effort to pronounce them. You may want to start by repeating these sentences and others you find as you read or hear others talk. The more you use this sound, more comfortable you'll be with it. By the way, in the final chapter of this book are tips to help you put all these ideas into implementation as you work toward your goal.

Oh, No! The Long O Sound

Carefully notice the next time you say a word containing the long "o" vowel. When properly spoken your lips will form a "w" at the end of the word. If you ever find it necessary to seek a word with this sound in a dictionary, you may notice that the reference book even adds the "w" at the end of the pronunciation.

In order to perfect your enunciation of words containing this sound, practice reading out loud either while you're alone or with a native English speaker. You may even want to have your friend read out loud first and then you parrot enunciating his words.

The following sentences all contain at least one word with the long "o" vowel.

I *hope* to go *home* Saturday.

Jane *rowed* the *boat over* to us.

Fred called *home.*

He had *hoped* his parents would *loan* him the money.

The only way to master this sound is to repeat it – as much as possible. By now this advice shouldn't come as much of a surprise: enlist the help of a friend you can trust, or use the internet or television.

The key is to pause the recordings and repeat them. In this way, you can see how close you can sound to the native speaker as possible.

The Long U Sound

The long U sound may be difficult to notice in the written language, but you'll have no trouble identifying it when you hear it. If, however, you're having difficulty pronouncing it like a native speaker, take your time and try to follow these instructions.

Begin with your jaw mostly closed. At the same time, place the top of your tongue close to your tooth ridge. From here, the sound changes into the "oo" sound we've mentioned previously.

You'll form this by performing two acts, one closely behind the other. First, close the lips forming a small circle. Immediately after that, you're lowering the tip of your tongue while raising the back of the tongue.

It's difficult sometimes to recognize when to pronounce the long "u" simply by looking at the spelling of a word. The spelling varies greatly word by word.

The following list of sentence should help you recognize when the long "u" is spoken.

Of course, the best way to learn this is through repetition. Here's the list:

My *shoes* are dirty.

I've lost my *toothbrush.*

The same *rules* hold *true* for you, *too.*

He was *introduced* to the largest *opportunity* of his career.

The *community* restricted the developer's plan.

The plan failed to receive the *approval* of city council.

What's the *use?*

Should we really be *doing* this?

If you've been practicing the suggestions and hints found in the previous chapters, they you can be assured you're well on your way of reducing your accent. But, there are still more methods you can learn to eliminate your accent. One of the ways is to learn about the soft palate. It's possible you may have never heard of this portion of your mouth.

If you are familiar with it, it's now time to reveal how to use it properly in order to get you one step closer to your dream job. Follow me to the next chapter.

Chapter 4: Considering the Soft Palate

You probably have heard of the soft palate, even though you may not know exactly what it is or even where it's located.

In simplest terms, it's the delicate piece of cartilage located between the roof of the mouth and what's known as the uvula. That's the fleshy extension that hangs in the back of your mouth.

If you're curious enough, you can place your finger in your mouth, touch your top teeth, then reach back a bit more. Now, you should be able to touch the gum. Don't stop here, though. Continue to reach up and back, past the roof of your mouth. You'll notice it feels a bit wetter and softer, the further back you go.

Congratulations! You've found your soft palate. Now, forget you even have it. Well, almost forget. This portion of your anatomy is the key factor why your voice may sound "nasal" when you speak. That nasal sound, in turn, may be causing your accent to be heavier than it needs to be.

That's because the palate is responsible for separating the oral cavity from the nasal cavity.

When you lower the soft palate, you allow air to pass through the nose via the nasal cavity. This causes you speak with a nasality – or a distinct nasal sound. If, though, the soft palate, remains in the original position, in which it would separate the nasal cavity from the oral cavity, air is trapped. In simple terms, the air can't travel through the nose.

If not the nose, where?

Instead of going up the nose, the air goes up through your mouth. This means you're producing a sound that's not nasal – as not as strong a nasal sound as when the soft palate is lowered.

It only seems logical that enunciating weaker vowel sounds would have the sounds traveling up the back of the throat and closer to the nasal cavity. This adds to the nasality of the sounds. Stop and think for a moment, if you will, where your vocal folds are located: They are positioned toward the front, close to the bottom of the mouth and in the throat.

When this occurs you're producing a nasal-like quality when you speak. You're lowering the soft palate during the course of your talking.

The goal is to sound less nasal. In order to do this, you'll want to consciously not lower your soft palate when speaking.

The most efficient way to do this is by speaking more from your throat or at a minimum, speak from the lower part of your mouth. Make a conscious effort not to speak through the upper portion of your mouth.

When you try this, you may be confronted with an Irrefutable law of nature: It seems impossible to speak without moving your soft palate – at least a bit.

Limited Jaw Movement

Before you say "there's nothing I can do to reduce this," I'm going to say, "Yes, there is." When you're not moving your jaw much, you're enunciating less and producing weaker vowel sounds. This could be a large part of your nasal sound which, in turn, contributes to your accent.

Your goal should be to produce vowel sounds that are stronger. In order to do this, you'll need to enunciate more clearly. You'll discover you'll have to work harder to produce the sound by moving your mouth and lips. In you do all of this, you'll be speaking with more definition. This may mean you'll need to adopt a slower speech pattern.

Speaking slowly general frustrates advanced English students like you. But be patient. It won't be something you'll need to do for a long time. Consider it a temporary trade off.

Another bone of contention for many individuals who speak English as a second language is that pesky "r" sound. Getting the pronunciation is a bit more difficult than many individuals believe. But it can be accomplished. Visit the next chapter to learn the way to do this.

Chapter 5: Learning about the "R" Sound: It's Trickier than you Think

It's called the hard "r" sound and it's hard in more ways than one. In fact, this sound is even a bit difficult for many native English speakers to conquer. I mentioned in the introduction. I spent at least one year in speech therapy in an attempt to learn the proper pronunciation of that sound.

I eventually conquered the sound, but to this day, if I'm tired, I'll mispronounce it.

Even though it may be tough, many instructors of English feel that the "r" sound is the "most important aspect of the American accent." No pressure here, now is there, to get this right?

You might also be interested in knowing that the hard American "r" is actually the only "r" worldwide that is distinctly considered a true hard sound. Yes, the Irish sound "aaR" comes in a close second.

In order to make this sound correctly, you'll move the tip of your tongue toward the back of your mouth, pointing it backwards and flex it.

The hard sound comes in three varieties: or, ar, and air.

We'll tackle the "or" sound first. Keep in mind, though, that if you can pronounce one, you'll eventually be able to pronounce all three. Just don't get discouraged. You'll also want to always keep in mind learning how to pronounce the "r" properly will go a long way toward reducing your accent.

Here are just a few examples of words with that "or" sound: floor, for, fork, order, ordinary, force, and remorse.

Of course, this is English so you can bet your bottom dollar that there are exceptions to this variety of spelling. Just a few of these include word, worm work, world and worst. Another variety of pronunciation can be heard in English as well, which is the "ore" sound. A few good examples of these include before, restored, more and shore.

Surprisingly, the same sound is often found in words spelled with the letter "a." Consider the words – all of these sounds, you'll notice follow the letter "w." These words include: swarm, war, warn, toward, and warrior.

Notice the difference, however, when the "e" follows the "war" sound as in warehouse, hardware and stare.

Yes, this can be a bit confusing. But as you study it more, it'll become second nature to you. The following sentences will all have the hard "r" sound in at least word. If you practice, you will conquer it. Guaranteed.

He placed his *order* with his server.

This is a *world* of *disorder.*

Many interpretations were *explored* in this book.

The *four* of them were searching for the *fork.*

The building looked *ordinary.*

We have *restored* the *floor* to its original elegance.

The *corners* of his mouth twitched.

May the *force* be with you.

Checking out the "ar" Sound

The sound of "ar" is produced, for the most part, when the combination of "a" and "r" are spoken together with no "e." Some of these words are quite simple, including: car, bar, far, Mars, darn, large, dark, arm, smart and remark.

Just when you think you may have found a pattern, the fact that you're studying English hits you square in the face. Here are a few words that are exceptions to the rule: backward, toward and forward.

If all this weren't enough, it's time to throw in one more exception. Take a good look at the word "our." Technically, it would be pronounced so it sounds like the vowel sound in power. But Americans, more frequently pronounce it with the "ar" sound.

Here are a few sentences to help you learn to how to perfect this sound.

I'm going to *our* car.

That's *our* only chance to claim what's truly *ours.*

Our meeting starts shortly

He was tall, *dark,* and handsome.

The *art* of writing letters has nearly disappeared.

She *startled* the intruder.

He gave her *harsh* glance.

He's a member of the *armed* services.

Exploring the "Air" Sound

Now that you're busy studying those typically American hard "r" sounds, we're about to move on to a slightly different sound, but still well within the definition of a hard "r." That's the "air" sound.

You'll discover this is more often sounded out like "ar" when it's followed by an "e," "y," or "i." Say these words out loud, or better yet, ask a native English speaker say the following few words out loud to get a better of idea of what I mean: care, share, scare, scares, barely, marry, rare.

The sound of "air" may show up with other spellings as well, most noticeably "ere" and "ear." Look at the words, wear and swear. Ask a native speaker to pronounce them for you or listen to them on an online dictionary which offers correct pronunciation of its entries. Be careful, though, because there are two common exceptions to this that immediately come to mind: were and ear.

Confusing? You bet. But you'll probably want to study and practice a bit and even enlist the help of native English speaking friends. Listen to someone recite these sentences, then repeat them after him or her.

I don't *care* what you think of me.

Do you know *where* Tony is?

I was *upstairs* most of the day.

I *swear* I don't know *where* she is.

The trick to pronouncing and sound like a native is to remember that all hard "r" sounds are short. Don't linger too long on that sound. Again, if you listen closely to native speakers, you'll at least have an idea of the sound you should be making when speaking these words. Then you can tackle it for yourself.

Chapter 6: Conquering the "th" sound

Just when you think the English language couldn't get much more confusing, we're moving from the hard "r" sound to the "th" sound. This is another aspect of the English language that frequently even gives native speakers a difficult time.

While I was in speech therapy for the "r" sound, my best friend was going through the same instruction, only for the "th" sound.

But, while it may be – dare I say – "foreign" to you, you'll soon be conquering the pronunciation of these two letters just as you have done with all the other tricky sounds we've thrown your way.

In this chapter, we're going to talk about the two subtle, yet different sounds these two letters make depending on the words in which they're included. Linguists refer to the two sounds as either "voiced" or "unvoiced."

The voiced and unvoiced "th" sounds are the only pair that actually use the same spelling – which, you can undoubtedly guess, only adds to the confusion. This sound is also problematic, because to be truthful, most Americans probably can't tell the difference most of the time. If we were to take the time to truly listen closely enough, we'd be able to detect. Before you're done reading this chapter you'll probably be able to tell the difference yourself. The next natural step then is to embrace the differences and conquer the sounds.

How to Pronounce these Sounds

As we mentioned the differences in sound are subtle. It should come as no surprise then that the way you pronounce them are also very much alike. Below are the basic instructions on how to get started for either sound.

First, you position the tip of your tongue behind the top of your front teeth. This ensures that when you go to pronounce this, you'll have generate the friction necessary for proper enunciation. Keep your lips relaxed.

An Alternative Method

There's also a second way to pronouncing this sound. In this method, you'll position the tip of your tongue between your top and bottom front teeth. If you find yourself using this method, you may also discover it makes it difficult to shift quickly to other sounds.

The reason for this is that your tongue needs to be so far in front when its placed between your upper and lower front teeth. You may not consider this much of a distance, but your tongue doesn't have quite the agility to move swiftly, either.

Consider this: Continuous Consonants

The other hint that is helpful in learning to pronounce either the voiced or unvoiced "th" sound is that they are what is known as "continuous consonants." This means that you should, under ideal conditions, be able to hold these sounds for a few seconds. Not only should you be able to hold them, but do so with in an even and smooth enunciation for the entire time. No pressure here, right?

The second aspect of these sounds are they're known as "fricatives," which means most of the sound is derived from the friction produced from the air traveling through that small opening in the vocal tract.

Now that we've have the technicalities of pronouncing these words correctly, it's time to show you the subtle difference between the sounds of the voiced and unvoiced "th."

The Good News about the "the" Sound

After everything you've learned about the "voiced" and "unvoiced" "th" sound, you may be a bit surprised to learn that there is even a spark of good news out there about it. Believe it or not, it's considered one of the most consistent sounds in the English language.

When you see the combination of letters together you can be sure that they are almost always pronounce it the same way. But English being what it is, does contain its exceptions in this sound as well. Consider, for example, the words, Thailand, Thomas and Thames all of which you'll pronounce with a "t" sound.

You'll also find that on occasion that the "th" is really a cluster of two consonants and you'll pronounce the "t" and "h" separately. This occurs most notably in compound words. Some of these include anthill, lightheaded, lighthouse and knighthood.

Examples of Voiced "th" Sounds

Here are few examples of the voiced "th" sounds. The voiced option can appear in any part of a word, the front, the middle or the end. I realize that makes it more difficult to recognize. In order to hear the difference and the proper pronunciation, as a native speaker to read these words to you: that, than they, though, themselves, therefore, therein, feather, together, bathing, father, mothing, clothing, weather, another, rather, soothing, tether, breathe, lathe. Seethe, loathe.

Just as with the voiced "th" sound, the unvoiced alternative can and does show up in any part of a word. The following is a list – of course, not complete – of the unvoiced "th" sound. Listen closely to a native speaker say these. Then try to imitate him or her as closely as you can.

They include: thorn, thin, think, thousand, thirsty, thief, thermometer, thaw, thread, thoughtful, three, thick, therapy, thimble, Thursday, bathtub, toothache, toothbrush, toothpaste, toothpick, marathon, python, healthy, truthful, wealthy, athlete, birthday, pathway, cloth, math, math, tooth, month, fifth, path, beneath, path, wreathe, broth, booth

Are You Making any of these Errors?

If the "th" sound is new to you, it may take some practice for you to learn the proper placement of your mouth, as well as listening to the correct sound. The good news is that while this is a difficult sound, there are a few ways that it's sometimes pronounced by non-native speakers. If you can identify one of these ways, then you may find it easier to correct and even perfect your pronunciation.

For the most part, those who speak English as a second language stay within the appropriate sound category. They substitute the voiceless "t" or "s" sounds for the voiceless "th." Similarly, they use the voiced "d" and "z" sounds for the voiced "th." Here are just a few ways these can manifest in your accent.

Many individuals end up saying "mouse" when they're trying to pronounce "mouth." They say the word "tree" for the word "three." They say "sink" for "think" and "bat" for "bath." You'll also hear the word "dare" for "there" and "ladder" for "lather."

If this sounds like you, then you're probably already working on this area. Don't be too upset if the pronunciation doesn't click with you immediately. Work on this area consistently and persistently. You'll be pleasantly pleased – and mildly proud – at how quickly you'll pick it up.

In the meantime, we'll talk about another portion of the English language which may be giving you a difficult time: diphthongs. Don't know what they are? You're not alone. In the next time, you'll discover what they are and how you can use them to speak like a native.

Chapter 7: Discovering Diphthongs

You say you've never heard of the word "diphthong" before? No problem.

Many native speakers have no idea what a diphthong is even though they use them every day. Probably many times throughout the day, in fact. The fact is that it's difficult to speak the English language without using diphthongs.

A diphthong is a single vowel sound that are composed of more than one vowel. It really is much easier to understand than you're thinking at this moment. This sound begins as one vowel sound and moves toward the next sound. When they're pronounced they are enunciated as one sound. Take the words coin for example. Your mouth begins as an "o" but as you form the "i" sound, it's pronounced as "oy."

Loud is also a good example of a diphthong. It, too, starts with an "o" sound, but then merges with the "u" to produce an "ow" sound that rhymes with "wow."

These two pronunciations stand in contrast to two vowels standing together in a word which retain their distinct vowel sounds. Words with these sounds are called monophthongs. The words violin, triage and chaos fall into this category. Notice that not only are the vowels are pronounced separately, but they also are split into separate syllables.

A Difference you can Feel

If you're unsure how you're pronouncing them, there is, believe it or not, a method you can use to test yourself. Place your index finger on both sides of your mouth. Next, say the short vowel sound of "a" (pronounced "ah"). Your fingers shouldn't move. Nothing happens. Why? Your fingers are motionless, because your mouth doesn't move during this. You'll discover this is the case with most of the vowel sounds.

This same test ends with different results when you pronounce the "oy," and "ow" sounds. When you place one index finger on each side of your mouth and make those sounds, your mouth should move. In effect, your mouth moves from making the first vowel sound to the next to create this sound.

Curiously (and I certainly don't mention this to confuse you), there are two other vowel sounds with actually pass the diphthong test. They aren't vowel consonants, but free-standing vowels: the long "i" and "a" sounds. If you place your index fingers on the side of your mouth, you'll discover that your mouth moves – because they are composed of two distinct sounds. Most linguists recognize these as diphthongs. Most reading teachers do not.

Here are a few of words that are pronounced as one sound, blending one vowel sound flawlessly into the other. This short list shows you the diphthong that is pronounced in the words, how and wow.

These include: cow, allow, owl, down, clown, drown, browser, browse, powder, proud, cloud, doubt, foul, noun, south, mouth, couch, found, around, amount, mountain, bounce, allowing, plowing, towel, bowel, hour, sour, flour.

The other diphthong we've mentioned is the "oy" sound as in the word boy. You'll discover that there are many words with these sound, some with different spellings. Here is a partial list -- and I do mean only a partial list: noise, voice, avoid, poison, join, point, foil, oil, spoil, exploit, toy, toying, annoy, employ, employing, employer oyster, destroyer.

Have I filled your head with enough rules and regulations – and exemptions to those same rules and regulations? Are you ready to say, "Enough!"

I have to admit you have enough material to master to take you along your journey to sounding like a native English speaker. In the following chapter, I'm ready to show you how to put it all together. Go ahead! Take a deep breath before you go there. You deserve at least that.

Chapter 8: Putting it All Together

For some individuals the idea or reducing or eliminating their accent appears like an insurmountable hurdle. Just when you think you can see the light at the end of the tunnel, you encounter a person who's been speaking it as their second language longer than you've been alive. The person is still speaking with an accent. What gives?

If they haven't eliminated their accent by now, how could you ever hope to? First, stop thinking like this. You can and will reduce your accent as long as continue to pursue this goal. Of course, there are some more effective ways and not-so-effective ways. This chapter lists some of the most efficient methods of putting everything you've learned up to this point and literally "putting it all together."

1. Watch television shows

When I talk to individuals how have successfully shed their accent, they confess that watching TV played a major role. Wow! I thought that impressive. I had never really thought as this being a viable option until a variety of people, with different first languages, kept telling me how much watching television helped them.

Why would that be so?

First, watching television is a safe way of studying what the English language is all about. Not only do you get to hear how it's spoken naturally, but you can also sample the idioms used within a safe environment. If you don't understand a phrase or a word you can either literally write it down later to discover the meaning or ask someone later.

Secondly, you'll develop an ear for the nuanced accent of the speaker and how you may then repeat it. If you can, watch television shows already pre-recorded on DVDs, so you can listen to them time and again and immerse yourself in the language and especially the accent.

2. National Public Radio as a Model

Perhaps there is no better model for perfecting the pronunciation of the English language that National Public Radio better known NPR. Even native-speaking English speakers are in awe of the powers of speech the typical host and reporter has.

3. Shadowing

This technique is highly recommended if you're either in your beginning stages or for individuals, like yourself, who are already advanced students trying to speak with less of an accent in order to be better accepted at work or within your study group.

If you've never heard of it before, the concept is simple. While you're listening to someone or something, like a television show or a National Public Radio broadcast, try to repeat – technically to shadow – what you've just heard. Do this as quickly as you can. By this, I mean to repeat it sentence by sentence. It doesn't matter if you repeat the entire story. The goal is to pick a sentence, repeat it. Then as soon as you have done that, repeat the next sentence you hear. t is one of the most beneficial ways to learn.

The only addition to this technique is to be walking swiftly while you're doing this. I wish I could answer why the walking and talking – when taken together work so well, but I can't. Many experts believe it may have some relation to receiving more oxygenation helps you to learn.

As a professional attempting to boost his ability to sound like a native speaker, you're probably ready just to jump in at the advanced shadowing. You can shadow an audio recording of a book or even a news talk show while you walk. If you're reading – and you're careful – consider walking and reading. This is problematic at times. But if he stay in your home and walk from room to room where you're comfortable maneuvering, it works nicely.

Those who have used shadowing as a method of acquiring a more American accent when speaking English, say that while it's effective, it's also a tedious, difficult method to accomplish.

I tell you this not to discourage you, but to warn you. The individual described shadowing as a "boring, grueling technique." He also said it was "about as much fun and as much work as weightlifting.

However painstaking this technique may be, he did offer this one bit of advice. Only perform shadowing one sentence at a time. Listen to the sentence; repeat the sentence. Listen to the sentence; repeat the sentence.

After all these caveats, he did admit that he didn't "know of any other effective way to reduce an accent with home study."

Keep in mind that reducing your accent may not always be easy, but if you remember all the reasons you're doing it – which may very well include a promotion or advancement in your career, you'll then realize the effort you exert is well worth.

4. What about Podcasts and YouTube?

There are primarily two ways you can put podcasts and YouTube to work for you in reducing your accent. The first is straightforward. Search the internet for podcasts and YouTube videos created specifically to give you advice on the topic. There are several good varieties. As you search, you'll discover the one that perfectly fits your needs.

The second method and is one frequently overlooked. Listen to a podcast or a YouTube video on a subject you enjoy. In this way, the subject matter will be able to keep your interest. Use these as a form of role modeling. Listen to them not only for content, but to immerse yourself in the English language. Imitate the way the native English-speaking participants talk.

Adopting a Role Model

This probably seems too simple to work. Many individuals have tried it and say that it works much better than they thought it would. This technique is just as it says. Select an individual who speaks English the way you would ideally like to. Be sure when you're searching for this "role model" that you select an individual you can trust.

Part of this exercise is that you're going to ask him or her to correct your English when he notices your accent getting heavier. Ask him if he'll work with you. Sometimes this means stopping an entire conversation and spending a few moments just working on a phrase or a word.

Your responsibility is to follow his instructions. Now you can see why you need to select an individual you can trust. Don't take offense when he corrects you, keeping in mind he's doing exactly what you asked of him.

The following chapter is all about reverse accent mimicry. This method, which is remarkably similar to the ones we've talked about in this chapter, actually takes the suggestions one step further.

To discover how more than one person has successfully reduced his accent using this remarkable imaginative method, all you need to do is to continue on to the next chapter.

Chapter 9: Reverse Accent Mimicry

Since your goal is to reduce your foreign accent, then you may want to explore the concept of *reverse accent mimicry.* It's not the simplest idea to understand, but it just may be an exercise that'll work for you. So I feel compelled to at least talk a bit about it.

The idea is that the quickest and easiest method of breaking through your accent and any pronunciation issues in your second language, in this case English, is by finding a person who speaks English as their first language and simply mimic their "accent" while you're speaking your own native language.

Think about it for a moment. When I first explored this concept, I had to allow the idea soak in for a while. In fact, when it was first explained to me, I wasn't even sure I fully understood the concept. But as I continued to explore the theory, it made sense to me.

In essence, you'll walk through four steps.

1. Find a "reverse model."

This is a person who speaks your native language with a thick accent based on the language you're attempting to conquer. Let's say your first language is French, but your goal is to speak flawless English. You're looking for someone who is comfortable speaking English but, still has his or her French accent.

I know right now, you're tempted to bail and move on to another chapter, but at this point stay with me, please.

2. Your goal is to mimic your model in your first language.

If you speak French, then ask this person to speak some in French. Don't just repeat what they say, mimic everything you notice in how they speak, down to their gestures. In a very real way parrot everything you can as well as you can about them when they speak.

If you're afraid you won't remember what your model is saying, then give him a monologue to read or a portion of a book to read. If it would make you feel more comfortable record a television show or watch one Netflix or Hulu. You can then just mimic these characters down to a tee.

3. Transition this mimicry into your second language.

The next step is to shift to mimicking this character or person, only this time in the second language. Yes, the language in which you're trying to reduce you accent. It's essential at this point that you keep everything as close to his "act" as possible. Don't change is animation, expression, pronunciation or even intonation. The only difference is that not you're speaking in the language you're learning – your second language. You'll discover that while you were mimicking your model, you almost subconsciously adopted much of the necessary native nuances of the language which are vital to learning a second language.

4. Finally, use one-on-one interaction with a speaker of your second language.

Preferably, you'll want this face-to-face time to be with a native English speaker. As you speak with him, you'll notice an immense reduction in your accent. Not only that, but you'll soon discover that others can hear it in your spoken word as well.

A friend of mine is a strong advocate of this method. His first language is English, but was trying hard to speak French like a native. Unfortunately, as he tells it his "carry-over English foreign accent" always got in the way. He explained that even though his French grammar and vocabulary were great, his listeners "often misunderstood me or asked me to repeat." Sound familiar?

He finally broke through that barrier, he told me, when he was in France watching the old movie Gigi, starring the legendary actor, Maurice Chevalier. The theater showed its original English version with French subtitles. After the movie was over, he began doing his impersonation of Chevalier, mimicking everything from gestures to the way he spoke English.

Without giving it a second thought, he was "effortlessly mimicking French prosodic melody and stress patterns," as he explained it to me. He said what he heard as he did this was his speaking with exaggerated and tenser French speech patterns. Without even knowing it he was using the French intonation and pronunciation qualities that had been so difficult for him to acquire up until then.

Furthermore, he continued to tell me excitedly, that he suddenly had the ability to use "a whole cluster of salient spoken French intonation and pronunciation qualities" that had before somehow eluded him.

Reverse accent mimicry could be a unique and enjoyable, even playful, way to reduce your foreign accent quickly. At the very least, you can give it a try. If nothing else, you'll have a good time. My bet is, though, that you'll find, just as my friend did, it could be the "superhighway" to reducing your accent.

He even confessed to me: "I discovered that from that moment on, my accent problems were nearly gone."

Give it a try. If it doesn't work for you, that's fine. But if it indeed does, then you've found the elusive "superhighway" to accent reduction. Congratulations.

The following chapter provides you with eight tips, tricks and techniques of squeezing in methods of accent reduction throughout your day. These are, for the most, part quick and easy.

The goal of these is to keep the need of accent reduction front and center in your consciousness. To discover these, simply continue reading to the next chapter.

Chapter: 10: 8 Secrets to Accent Reduction

If you're as serious about reducing your accent as I believe you are, then you're probably already implementing quite a few of the methods explained in the previous chapters. In addition to those, I'd like to share with you eight secrets of accent reduction that most individuals don't think to share with you. It's not that they're purposely keeping these tips, tricks and techniques from you. It's that they may have stumbled across them in their search for shortcuts to accent reduction.

Test out the following tips. If they work for you great!

1. The English language has a unique cadence.

Some have compare the cadence of English to that of jazz music. Think about how in that genre one note sometimes flows effortlessly into the other and how the intonation of the music changes at a moment's notice.

Many students, new to the English language, are naturally careful in their speech, fearful of making a mistake. They speak slowly and carefully with pauses between every word. This, for a native, is a telltale sign that English isn't your first language. So many English words are connected. Consider the phrase "How are you?" The first two words are said almost as if they were one.

Another good example of this is the phrase "got you." For some reason, native speakers string this together to make it sound like one word. On top of that, they also place a "tch" sound in there. In effect, it sounds more like "gotchya" than anything else.

The point is that if you deliberately separate every word you speak, you'll sound stilted and robotic. The next time hear someone speak English, pay attention to this aspect of the language.

2. Listen to audiobooks.

Without a doubt, this is one of the best ways to reduce your accent. Not only that, but it's a "safe" method. While you listen to these native speakers in the privacy of your car or home, you'll be able to get the feel for all the nuances that go into the English language. In effect, this secret trains your ear to actually "stop hearing with your accent," which can be critical to your ultimate success.

3. Detect when an "s" is really a "z."

What? There really are times in the English language that we write the word using the letter "s" but end up saying the word as if it were a "z." Go figure.

You'll find this occurs, more often than not, when the "s" is the final letter of the word. Knowing when to use the "z" sound and when not to will help you reduce your accent. Listed below are just a few words illustrating this example.

In the following words the final "s" sounds like a "z" when spoken: beds, cries, rays. The next three words end in the letter "s" and are pronounced as an "s": bells, hits, tacks.

4. Learn to detect "voiced" sounds from "unvoiced" ones.

Many consonants in the English language are only spoken as voiced. These include, "b," "d," "g," "l," "m," "n," "ng," "r," "v," "w," "y," and "z." Quite a long list, isn't it?

We've talked about this in regard to the "th" sound, which has a slight difference to its sound whether it's voiced or unvoiced. What we didn't mention, however, is the fact that there are a few others, including the "h," "k," "p," "t," "s."

Here's another way to tell whether the words below have a voiced or unvoiced consonant. Place your index and middle fingers at the hollow of your neck. The closer to the base of the neck you can put it, the more accurate you'll be at identifying the sound. If the sound is voiced, there'll be no vibration there. If you do feel a vibration then you'll know the sound is unvoiced.

In each pair of words, one is voiced and the other not. Practice distinguishing one from the other:

bad/bat	rod/rot
lab/lap	tab/tap
bag/back	beg/beck
bus/buzz	lace/laze

5. Record yourself speaking English.

Yes, record yourself, but don't stop there. Take a sentence or two and record yourself. Then play it back and write down what you said. Here's the catch, though, don't write it as it's correctly spelled. Transcribe it phonetically. Let's say you recorded yourself speaking the sentence: "I think the bed is too soft." What you hear when you transcribe this is "I dink da bet iss doo sof."

If that's what you hear, write it down. Look for errors. In this example we know the "th" sound came out as a "d" and the voiced sounded more like a voiceless "t." Additionally the "z" sound in the word is sounded more like an "s" and the final "t" in soft was actually dropped.

This is one of the best ways that you can evaluate yourself. Of course, the key is to keep using this method while at the same time listen to native speakers to help you overcome these errors.

6. Buy a Pronunciation Dictionary

This can be one of the most valuable things you can do. If you've never heard of one before, it's exactly what it sounds like. In addition to giving you the proper pronunciation, this type of dictionary also helps you with discover the proper stress and how to break the word into syllables.

You can find them in just about any bookstore. If you have trouble finding it, ask a clerk; she'll know exactly what you mean. Some varieties of this dictionary may even come with an audio CD so you can easily listen to the correct pronunciations.

7. Practice, practice, practice.

Perhaps this secret isn't quite what you expected. It will, however, make the difference between speaking with or without an accent. The fact is that unless you use the English language, you'll never be able to speak it without your native accent. Give yourself time to learn the pronunciation. Don't think that you'll lose your accent overnight. If you practice, though, you will eventually speak more like a native.

This happens, if for no other reason, you're practicing the correct placement and movement of your tongue.

8. Learn the art of message chunking

The art of what?

I can hear you ask that now. It's called message chunking and it's a habit many native English speakers have. To sound truly native, your delivery of English need to be broken into "clear and logical" breaks of words, commonly called chunks. These are often referred to as thought groups.

In English, an average thought group is approximately three to four words long. At the end of each of these thought groups, native English speakers insert a pause. It's only a split second long, but if you listen close enough you can hear it. They're called thought groups because they are a chunk of words that can stand alone and still make sense. They're similar to a short portion of a much longer sentence. If you choose the wrong time to pause, like in the midst of one of these thought groups, you'll discover your listeners have a difficult time following your train of thought.

Not only that, but within each of these chunks of thoughts, there should be a single word that takes on the main emphasis. This is the word that needs to be stressed or emphasized when you speak. It may take a while to discover exactly where to stop to create these chunks of messages. With enough practice, though, you'll soon know nearly instinctively how to create effective and intelligent thought groups.

You may not think this is a big deal, but give it a try. You'll be surprised at how much your accent disappears.

Even if you only implement a few of these eight tips, you'll be making great strides in reducing your accent. When you put these tips together with the previous suggestions and directions found in all the other chapters, you've found a remarkable and nearly unbeatable road to sounding more like a native speaker of English daily.

Conclusion

Congratulations! You have learned the most important tools needed to effectively reduce your foreign language and make great strides in acquiring one that sounds more closely to a native English speaker.

Having said that, I'm sure you realize you probably haven't mastered any of these techniques – yet, that is! – nor do you sound like you have spoken English since the day you were born.

But, if you continue to study these, practice them on a daily basis and keep some of these tips, tricks and techniques in your consciousness, then you've taken some of the most important steps toward making it so.

If, prior to reading this book, you felt as if there were no hope for you in ever accomplishing this, then my sincere desire is that we've lifted your expectations that it really is possible to do so. You've heard many people from other countries talk fluently and flawlessly in English – without the accent. If they can do it, so can you.

You'll naturally want to re-read certain sections of this book, depending on what presents the most trouble for you. I encourage you to. In this way you can work on the most stubborn aspects you're encountering.

There are plenty of methods other than what I've just presented here. These, though, I've discovered are among the quickest and most relevant one. I'm quite sure you'll find more ways to do this than what I could list here. If so that's great. Just keep in mind that for the most part, you'll want to listen carefully to those who were raised with English as their first language.

If you're planning on being successful, you'll have to put yourself on the line at times and ask those native-speaking individuals you know to help you overcome your accent. You'll discover that there are many people who would not only be glad to help you in your quest, but would probably be honored as well.

A Tedious Job

I've quoted one friend who described overcoming his accent as being as tedious and boring as lifting weights. For some that may be so. Keeping this in mind, try to meet this goal with a smile, knowing that in the end, all the effort and "weightlifting" is worth it. Because it is.

There's not a place or sentence in this book in which I've promised shedding your accent and adopting one closer to a native speaker of English would be easy. You, however, already knew that. If it were easy, you wouldn't need any guidebook.

So as much as you dream of waking up one day and waving a magic wand that allows you to speak perfect English accent-free, it's not going to happen that way. It will, however, occur and with less pain than you may think, when you develop the habit of speaking English and listening to native speakers on a daily basis.

Don't worry that you may not be able to learn it in person. Take your education whichever way works. By this I mean that the internet opens new vistas generations prior to us never had.

In previous generations, meeting native speaking individuals of a language was about the only way to shed your own accent. You had to be lucky enough to visit the country or happen to run into one in your country.

Today, you can turn on the television, cruise the internet, watch Netflix and so much more. Many of them, by the way, can be accomplished in a "safe" environment – one in which you needn't fear about anyone making light or teasing you about your accent.

It's up to you to take advantage of these amazing methods as best you can.

Continue working toward your goal. The sky's the limit.

Thank you for reading "Accent Reduction For Professionals".

I sincerely hope that you received value from this book and gain a better understanding of how you can gradually reduce your accent.

If you enjoyed this book, please take a moment to share your thoughts and leave a review on Amazon, even if it's only a few lines; it would make all the difference and would be very much appreciated!

As a gift for reading this book, I would like to share 3 Chapters of "English Fluency For Advance Speaker" to you. I hope you will enjoy it.

Whitney

Nelson

Bonus

Chapter 1: Getting Over the Plateau to Become a Fluent English Speaker

Are you frustrated? Do you believe you've hit the peak of your learning with regard to the English language? You can read the language. You know the grammar and you can understand it when you hear the spoken word.

Yet, you're not speaking it as fluently as you want to – as you need to. No, there's nothing wrong with you. Many persons learning English feel as you do. They've reached a certain point in their ability to speak the language and just can't seem to advance any farther.

Unfortunately, they believe that what they've learned is all that they *can* learn. They've tried and tried to reach that next level fluency but to no avail.

Does this sound like your story? Are you ready to throw up your hands and give up, thinking any more progress is hopeless? Don't quit.

But before you continue any farther, stop knocking your head against the wall. Obviously what you're doing right now is not working. It's time to step back and analyze what needs changed in your approach to learning.

Instead of going any further in your pursuit of learning the spoken English language, you need to look into your own thinking to discover if you're holding any "limiting beliefs" holding you back. These are really myths that many people hold as the truth about their ability to learn to speak English fluently that, quite frankly, just aren't true.

Here are five of the most common limiting beliefs that students of English believe are natural barriers to their learning. These "beliefs" which many attribute to holding them back from being a more fluent speaker are really nothing more but preconceived notions. They can be overcome simply by changing your thinking. Then you can break that barrier to attain the next level of fluency. It may sound a bit strange, but it really does work.

5 Myths That May Be Hindering Your English Fluency

1. Your age

This is just an excuse. At one time scientists believed that as persons aged, the harder it was for them to learn. And not just the English language, everything – math, science even the adopting of new hobbies like knitting or playing the piano.

If you think about it, that's a pretty dismal diagnosis. The standard scientific thought stated that your brain cells continued to reproduce and were receptive to learning only up to a certain age. Once you reached that age your body would no longer make any new cells. If you could learn anything new, it would be much more difficult, taking a longer period of time. Whatever it was you wanted to learn, the scientists warned you it would be an uphill battle.

The lesson people took from this dictum? If you didn't learn a language when you were younger, well you were out of luck. You weren't about to learn it as an older individual. If you did manage it, you'd be struggling every step of the way.

Today, scientists have discovered that proclamation – taken as a law for so long – is not in the least bit true.

You need to know right now that your age doesn't limit your ability to speak English fluently. It's more likely you believing your age is a limiting factor actually keeps you from learning. Once you overcome this mindset, you'll discover that English isn't as difficult to speak as you thought – and before you know it you've unlocked the secret that has prevented you from going any further.

It's time to stop blaming your age for that plateau you've reached to learn and start using the English language more. With the suggestions presented throughout the rest of this book, you'll discover that it's easier than you once believed.

2. Fear of making mistakes.

Many individuals refuse to speak English as often as they could. Why? Simply because they're afraid of making mistakes. But worse than that they believe that someone will hear them make these mistakes and laugh at them.

The thought of making a mistake when speaking English shouldn't inhibit you or limit your speaking it in any way. In fact, it really should do the exact opposite – it should spur you on to speak it all the more.

Deep down you already know what I'm about to tell you: mistakes are your friends. Making a mistake when you talk is the ultimate way to learn the English language or any language for that matter.

Every single person learning a language made some type of mistake when they started. In fact, if the truth be known, they made what they considered more than their fair share of blunders. Even native speakers don't speak perfect English. Listen closely to some native speakers and you'll see exactly what I mean.

What if I told you that instead of fearing those mistakes, you should be embracing them? Would you think I was totally insane? Well, that's exactly what you should be doing –

speaking more and making more mistakes. That's because the more mistakes you make, the faster you'll learn.

Let me tell you a story about two individuals, both learning English. Both, in fact, were at about the same level of fluency. They could read and comprehend English well and in general had a good grasp of speaking it. Both wanted to go beyond where they were currently and hit the next level of fluency.

But one student feared speaking it, not only in her daily life, but also in the classroom. She would never volunteer in class and when called upon she would barely speak up. When she did answer, she used as few words as possible. The instructor continually asked her to expand on her answers.

The other student, coincidentally, was in the same classroom, and took every opportunity to speak English. He was the student always first to volunteer to answer in English. Instead of just answering with a short phrase or a one-word answer, he would make sure he'd elaborate a bit more – sometimes more than he needed to. The point is that he took every opportunity in class to speak English.

Not only that, but he would make sure he used the language as much as possible outside of the classroom as well. He made a concerted to associate with people who spoke English and made it a point to speak up in conversations even. If someone corrected his English, he thanked them. He would go on to explain that he was still learning and appreciated the corrections.

You could tell in an instant that the first student shied from talking because she feared making mistakes. She believed that every word that came out of her mouth had to be perfect. The second student, though, approached his learning not only as a positive activity, but something that was actually fun. Making mistakes didn't bother him.

You can guess who learned to speak English more quickly and more fluently. Don't let fear of making mistakes – either in class or in public – hold you back from speaking the language. We've all made mistakes – whether we're learning a language or math or any other subject. Mistakes are the foundation of any type of learning.

3. You can't remember all the rules of grammar.

Wow! Definitely don't let this hold you back. No one, not even native speakers, can remember all the grammar rules. In fact, few speakers even try to follow all the rules. This includes native English speakers. If you took the time to review all the grammar that went into speaking a sentence before you spoke it, you'd never utter another English sentence.

Instead, place your faith in your vocabulary and especially listening to others. And if you make it a point to speak English, stop holding yourself to some impossible standard; you'll never ever enjoy the language. Belief it or not, learning a new language is fun – really fun.

Perfect grammar is the last thing you need to worry about. Instead, spend your time expanding your vocabulary, learning new words and using them as much as possible in conversations. Speak English every chance you get – whether you're clear about the grammar involved in the sentences you used or not.

This book is all about speaking the English language fluently. It's not about learning grammar. It's about using the language. Let's say that you're in a group of people and want to say that you ate an apple yesterday. If your grammar is shaky you may say "I yesterday apple eat."

Don't worry about making a fool of yourself. A native speaker may correct you and tell you the sentence is structured like this: "I ate an apple yesterday." Poof! You've learned to speak the language a little better through speaking up. And now you actually have a pattern for speaking a sentence like that.

You've learned first how to pattern a sentence in the past tense. You've also learned that the past tense of eat is "ate." In that small insignificant mistake, you've broken through to the next level.

And the best part is that you didn't have to struggle over any grammar rules. All in all, you probably now feel better about yourself. Not only for speaking up but for actually learning how to use English grammar at the same time. Imagine how quickly you can improve your grammar without even thinking about it just by speaking a few sentences. Imagine what would happen if you spoke even more.

Instead of holing yourself up in your house and studying the dizzying array of grammar rules before you speak, get together with English speakers – native speakers and students like yourself – and use the vocabulary you've already learned.

4. You need to travel to be able to speak English fluently.

Another fallacy. You don't need to travel anywhere in order to improve your speech. There are many people who have learned the English language without going very far from home. If you're already living in the United States, that's not so much an issue, anyway.

But if you're currently living outside an English-speaking country and learning the language with an eye to visiting such a country in the near future you may view learning English is a hopeless pursuit. You may also be re-assessing why you're even bothering to learn the language.

Don't start second-guessing yourself. You can learn the language from wherever you are at the moment even if you don't have access to what you think you need. Have access to a computer? Then you already know how many video clips are on the web in English. Listen to these, repeat what these speakers say and the way they say it. Imagine these speakers are in the same room with you.

If you have to, stop the video and repeat what they've said, then double check yourself. There are plenty of ways of learning English – and as long as you're learning, there is no wrong way.

The key here is to focus on learning it using a method that's available for you. Instead of mourning that you can't travel or you don't know anyone who is speaking the language, dig around on the internet and find an English-speaking site. You may even discover a site that teaches you English. There are certainly plenty out there.

5. There are no other people around me speaking English.

This is a corollary to the "I can't travel to an English speaking country" myth. While it certainly would be easier if you knew individuals who could speak English, it's definitely not essential – regardless of what you've heard to the contrary.

With a computer keyboard at your fingertips, and the internet, it doesn't matter whether you live with or next door to English speakers or not. With less effort than you'd ever imagine on your part, you can find someone who speaks English.

Not only that, I'm betting that you'll also discover students of English – just like yourself – who are looking for others who speak at their level of fluency. Imagine how much you all could help each other. Imagine how much you can learn with only a bit of effort on your part.

These are the five most common complaints that people use to block their excelling at speaking the English language like a native. How many of these apply to you?

What Are Your Personal Myths?

Do you have any other personally limiting beliefs that hold you back from learning to speak the English language? If you do, why not stop right now and write them down. Now study them really well. Are those really valid reasons for not learning the English language? Can you think of any way you can overcome them?

Regardless of what your personal thoughts are about your inability to get to the next level of English fluency, remember that the only thing that is holding you back are your beliefs. The moment you believe you can learn to speak the English language like a native, you will.

It's time to think more positively about your ability to improve your ability to speak the English language. Just changing your thinking from "Wow! This is really difficult," to "Hey, this is getting easier all the time!" will help you speak more fluently. Guaranteed.

Chapter 2: Setting S.M.A.R.T. Goals -- The Secret of Getting What You Want When You Want It

Pedro complained to his English instructor one day that he was disappointed that his fluency in the language seemed to have hit a peak. "I can't advance any farther," he said, "and I'm far from sounding like a native speaker. And that is the long run is my goal. Did I set my sights too high?"

The instructor told him that, indeed, he did not set any goal that he could not accomplish; he just may have to re-think how to reach them. That's when he told Pedro about S.M.A.R.T. goals.

Are you feeling "stuck" in your level of learning? Are you, like Pedro, beginning to think you'll never break through to that next level of learning in which you sound more fluent – more like a native speaker?

Then perhaps it's time you look into using S.M.A.R.T. goals as well. What are they? What make SMART goals different from any other? Simple. When you create this type of goal, you're strategically placing yourself in a position of achieving them. If you follow the guidelines of these techniques, in fact, it would be extremely difficult to fail.

S.M.A.R.T

I can hear you now, "When do we start?" Well, there's no time like the present. S.M.A.R.T. is an acronym for Specific, Measurable, Attainable, Responsible and Time-Bound. If you make your goals in accordance with these five guidelines, you're well on your way to fulfilling your English-language dreams.

But more than that, this is a technique used by a growing number of business executives as well as entrepreneurs to move their projects forward. It's time tested. And the best part is that you can take these guidelines and use them for any goals you have for your life.

The letter "S" in S.M.A.R.T. stands for specific. You've probably created many goals in your life. Think back to several of them. Think about the times you succeeded as well as those instances in which you didn't reach them. What made the difference? What did you do right when you achieved your goals? How did this differ from the times you didn't reach your dreams?

Perhaps it could be that the ones you achieved were worded more specifically. Did you know exactly what you wanted? This works regardless of what your goals are—they aren't necessarily related to your learning the English language.

Take, for example, the individual who wanted to lose weight. She started out by saying that "someday" she'd like to lose weight. But until she decided specifically how many pounds she wanted to lose, her weight held steady. Once she made the decision and gave herself a deadline, however, she couldn't understand why she couldn't stick to an eating plan.

So your first step is deciding specifically what it is you want to do. Once you know exactly what it is, then create specific steps you believe will get you there. Let's say your goal is to be able to speak English well enough to make a presentation in front of your supervisors and several department managers at work..

Now write down what you believe you need to do in order to speak English well enough to do it. These are your steps for reaching your goals. For example, if giving a presentation is the goal, you must look critically at your spoken language skills now.

Decide what type of improvements you need to make. You may decide you

- Want to work on your pronunciation
- Learn more vocabulary words – as well as perfect their pronunciation
- Learn how to tell a joke in English

What else do you believe is keeping you from reaching this level of fluency in the English language. Not sure? Ask your instructor or a trusted friend.

Make sure you keep a list of these, because you'll going to need them for the next step. Keeping in mind your goal of making this presentation, we'll go to the next step in S.M.A.R.T. goals

The M in S.M.A.R.T. goals stands for measurable. That may be a no-brainer when it's said that way, but you'd be surprised how many people create goals without thinking about how they're going to measure their progress. And if you can't measure whether you're a quarter of the way to your goal or half to making your dream come true, how will you ever know when you've reached that particular goal?

That's why you need to discover a way to measure your progress. Let's continue with the example we used in the previous paragraphs. You want to perfect your ability to speak English so you can give a presentation at work.

The first thing we listed that needed to be improved was your ability to pronounce English.

Let's say this is your goal as well. Just saying it doesn't get it done. You could spend years perfecting it, but never recognize when your speech is, indeed, good enough. Your first decision – and creating a measurable goal – is to either recognize your improvement yourself or getting someone's opinion on your pronunciation. Ideally, this would be your instructor or a trusted friend.

You see how by adding this idea of measuring your improvement, you've created a goal you can work toward – and feel good about attaining once you've reached it.

Your second step in speaking English well enough to make a presentation was expand your vocabulary. Here again you need to set a certain number of words you want to learn and to pronounce. If you don't settle on how many words, you could be learning words forever. So not only settle on how many, but perhaps pick out a few from an English book, or ask your English teacher for recommendations on a few words. You may even want to ask a few colleagues what type of words they would recommend that may be business related.

Within this, you'll then want to start tackling this list. In addition to having friends and tutors help with your pronunciation, remember the web – especially any dictionary applications or sites you have access to. The definition each entry provides you with a proper pronunciation of the word.

And finally one of your goals was to be able to tell a joke. How are you going to turn this into a measurable goal? You may want to practice in front of the mirror or with a good friend who'll be honest with you. Once you've earned the thumbs of a friend you may want to take your joke to several more people to get their opinions.

The key to success in creating any successfully measurable goal is to look at the details of what needs to be done and honestly evaluate your ability to do it. Making the decision on how to measure your progress is a big step in ensuring this will work.

While you should never give up your dream, you also need to be open to the process of making it measurable as well as creating the best possible strategy to make this happen You also need to continually reassess how vital these goals are to you.

Now that you have one or more goals that are specific measurable, your next step is to ensure that your goals are attainable   Yes, the A in S.M.A.R.T. goals stand for attainable.

This is an important aspect of creating any goal – not just those related to your speaking English. This step may take some time. First, you need to be absolutely honest with yourself. What do you truly believe you can attain. Don't overstretch your reach and set some impossible goal that is beyond your level. That will only disappoint you and you may wrongly believe learning English is simply beyond your capability.

It's better to set a goal and break it into two steps and reach it than set one that's simply impossible to reach. Let's face it I'm five foot two inches tall. If my goal were to play professional basketball that may be seen as an unattainable goal. But to set a goal that I make so certain percentage of the shots I take on the court is attainable for me. That goal involves more my skill more than my natural height.

Pedro, for example, originally set a goal of learning how to pronounce fifteen new words a week. Before he committed himself to that goal, though, he thought long and hard if it really were attainable. Having second thoughts, he instead set his sights on learning ten – at least for the first week. After that, he would adjust his goal depending on how he performed the first week.

When you're working with the idea of whether your goals are attainable, you may have to be flexible. If you discover that you set your sights a bit too high, reduce them. There's no shame in doing that. In fact, having a desire that is at least realistic will help build your self-confidence.

On the other hand, you don't want to make your target so easy that it doesn't challenge you. If your goal is too easy, you won't push yourself to do your best – and you may even lose interest.

Pedro may also want to create an attainable goal that he can meet with a teacher or close friend weekly to help him with his speaking. Once a week, for example, sounds reasonable. If he set his sights on meeting with someone five times a week that may be a bit excessive and end up being something he couldn't achieve – which would possibly make him feel as if he failed. In reality, he really didn't fail, he simply underestimated the time involved in meetings like that.

Pedro gave much thought to how to perfect telling a joke and the attainability of that goal as well. He admired several comedians on television. The question he had to ask himself was should he hold himself up to a professional level of delivery when he wasn't even a native speaker.

The fact of the matter was that he admired the presentations of several of his colleagues who had told some great jokes. The attainable goal, then, would be to practice until he felt he could present more like them. He thought that would be an attainable goal.

He could learn to pitch these jokes through various ways – including professionals on television as well as the colleagues you work with. Pedro also recorded himself telling the joke to review his pronunciation.

Not only does Pedro have to learn to be flexible, he has to discover what smaller, equally attainable, goals he break this dream into smaller chunks.

The letter R in S.M.A.R.T. goals stands for the word responsible. The question becomes who is responsible for achieving this goal. The obvious answer is Pedro. As you create your goals, it will become quite apparent that you are ultimately responsible. What Pedro learned as he went along, however, was he needed to hold those who offered services of their help responsible as well.

He would have difficulty attaining some of the goals without the help of his friends, colleagues and instructors. This by no means absolves him of all responsibility for achieving them, but it does mean he may have to ensure in some from that those who offered to help him actually do.

If that should occur, he may have to take the imitative in reminding his instructor or others that they had volunteered to help. He may have to suggest times they could meet. Pedro can't – and neither can you – just ask for help and then expect them to always take the initiative to help you.

Other issues that may fall under the responsible portion of the S.M.A.R.T. goals include the amount of time you can realistically invest in each goal. Hold yourself responsible for ensuring you've created goals that over extend you or your resources. If you set unrealistic goals, you'll be disappointed and tempted to give up.

You'll also have to approach your goals responsibly. A large part of that is knowing when to ask for help. It could be that you need someone to spend time with you and assess your pronunciation. It could also be something as simple as an individual who you report to occasionally who holds you accountable for your progress.

The T of the acronym of S.M.A.R.T. represents the phrase time-bound. Have you ever heard the saying that goals without a deadline are dreams? While it's admirable to have dreams, the word itself implies that it's something that you'll see fulfilled in the future. Or worse yet something that's totally unachievable.

You're not dealing with pie-in-the-sky dreams that you don't expect to come true. Not by a long shot. You're creating specific targets that you expect to reach. When can you expect to see these goals manifest? That's up to you.

One thing is one hundred percent certain, though: if you don't hold yourself to a deadline, they'll never materialize. Pedro discovered this. He found that if he didn't put a specific time to reach his goal, he was far less likely to actually achieve them.

Pedro, for example, knew that it would take some time before he would be able to master the English language well enough to present a project report to his colleagues at work. So he set his sights on achieving them in one year.

But he also knew that he had to do the same thing with the intermediate goals that would eventually get him to his dream. So he sat down with pencil and a calendar in order to start assigning a timeline to his smaller goals.

In order to do this correctly, he needed to analyze the smaller goals and set an attainable time line for all of his goals. The moment he realized that he would be running behind on one of the smaller aims, he then would need to re-evaluate all the goals which followed. It could mean that he would encounter a chain reaction. All the steps after that one would also be met later than he had intended.

If he encountered this, he could handle this is two ways. First, he could just delay the attainment of these steps and assignment himself a later manifestation day. Or, he could adjust his goals – even if it means working a bit harder and longer – in order to reach his ultimate goal on time.

The point of setting specific completion dates is that it helps you to plan. Pedro set a final target date as one year. A year from the day he started he hoped to be standing in front of his colleagues informing them about the progress of a project. If he saw he was falling behind on this timetable, he could then adjust his intermediate steps to recover some of the lost time.

Being held time-bound for a goal is also a great motivating factor to aid in your planning. Once Pedro set a final goal, he worked backwards in planning deadlines for all the smaller steps. He started with his final goal date and carefully charted where he had a be a month before his final goal and then two months before that date.

He actually spent quite a bit of time figuring out how much time he'd need for all the smaller steps needed in order to get where he wanted to be on time.

Pedro decided that in a week he should work on one lesson on vocabulary – learning the meaning of the words. Additionally, he needed to put in two practice sessions on pronunciation. One of those would be conducted on his own with the help of a recorder and the internet and one would be – when possible – with his instructor or a good friend.

The final decision Pedro made in fulfilling the time bound portion of the S.M.A.R.T. goals was to take a few moments periodically in order to assess his progress. He set his assessment dates as once a month. He compared where he was to where he hoped to be. Was he on track? Would he be able to make his goal within the time frame he set? Or was he running behind?

Did he need to increase the number of vocabulary words he was learning every week or did he need more work on his pronunciation. Whatever he eventually decided, he fine-tuned his schedule to accommodate his ultimate completion date.

S.M.A.R.T goals are an excellent method of ensuring you don't lose sight of your desires. How many times have set New Year's resolutions only to find by February, you realize you're not working toward them? That's because you didn't apply the follow up work necessary to keep you laser focused on your goal. You merely wrote down some vague goal and went on with your life. Your New Year's resolutions become nothing more than afterthoughts as you continued on with your life.

You can easily see how setting – and maintaining – S.M.A.R.T. goals are essential in manifesting your desire to speak English fluently. The key to working these goals is to keep them uppermost in your mind. Pedro learned – and so you'll discover this as well – that learning English is a daily discipline. You can't learn to speak fluently by cramming a week's worth of work into a day or two.

The Need for Flexibility

The other lesson Pedro learned from instituting this technique is that he needed to maintain a degree of flexibility. If a step isn't working, then he needed to revise it. If he hadn't progress as far as he had hoped by the end of a month or so, he needed to re-assess his strategy. He needed to analyze what was working and what wasn't. and he needed to do it on a regular basis.

But there is one more action Pedro took when he successfully completed each of his smaller goals. He rewarded himself. At the very least, he stopped for a few moments and told himself how good he was doing. Sometimes, he would treat himself to a dinner out or buy himself a small present.

You should consider doing something similar. It needn't be a large purchase or even a huge dinner. The important thing is that you stop for several moments and compliment yourself on doing a good job. Then cheer yourself on to going all the way.

Once you've set your goals, it's time to move on to learning methods on achieving these goals. In the next chapter you'll learn that the fastest way to learn English is to just dive into the language. You'll also learn some techniques on doing just that.

Chapter 3: Immerse Yourself in the English Language

Have you ever wondered what the difference is between an individual who seems to glide through learning the English language and someone who struggles with every word – perhaps even every syllable?

You may have assumed that's it a matter of skill. You dismiss their success as a natural talent they possess for learning the spoken word. You may even credit them with being smarter than the average person.

Well, you may think all of that, but you'd be wrong. Those who learn how to speak English fluently are neither smarter than you nor do they necessarily have a gift for learning languages.

What separates those who learn the spoken word of English from those who don't can be described in one word: immersion.

What? Those who seem to learn effortlessly simply immerse themselves into the language. They seek out opportunities to speak English at every turn. If they have to make a choice between speaking their native language or English, they choose English every chance they get.

Consider this for a moment. You'll never improve at any activity – jogging, playing piano or even knitting – unless you practice. Practicing the English language is the only way to immerse yourself in the language.

The Only Way to Learn English

Believe it or not, you can be the person who others envy at your quick grasp of the English language. You can be the individual who speaks it with ease. And you can start right now. As long as you keep these guidelines in mind.

1. Don't spend a lot of time perfecting your grammar.

Believe it or not, this is probably *the most important rule in learning how to speak English.*

Your goal isn't to write a paragraph in English with no grammatical mistakes. You goal is to speak it. So don't obsess with grammar. If you listen closely to native speakers not everyone speaks English perfect all the time.

Let's face it, at this point in your studies you already have a firm grasp of English grammar. You probably could even correct a native speaker when they don't use proper grammar. So, if your goal is to become a better speaker you need to focus on using it as if it were your first language.

Actually, studying grammar will only hinder your development using the spoken word. If you analyze what you're about to say and think about all the grammar rules before you speak, you'll discover the precise moment to say what you wanted to.

When you're thinking about this guideline you need to know that even most native speakers of the English language only know about 20 percent of all the hundreds (and hundreds) of the rules. A mere 20 percent. At this point in your studies, you probably already know more than that.

Don't worry, the more frequently you speak English, you'll undoubtedly get an ear for proper grammar. After a while, the sound of an improperly structured sentence or verbs that don't agree with you subject will sound horrible. As long as you know what sounds right, you'll be able to speak it well enough. I'm guessing that, as an advanced student, you already have a grasp of this aspect of your learning.

2. Learn phrases, not words.

Think about it. You probably know many vocabulary words. And you undoubtedly know how to pronounce them. But what you really need to study at this point are phrases. While knowing the words are, indeed, important, languages are really a compilation of phrases.

I'm sure you know students of the language who have an impeccable grasp of vocabulary words but still can't create a sentence if their life depended on it. Why? They failed to study English phrases.

When children learn how to talk, they're definitely immersed in their native language. It's usually the only language they hear from the moment they wake up until they're tucked into bed at night. What they hear are not separate words, but sentences, phrases and everything in between.

If you already know about 1,000 words (and you probably know more than that right now), you could still find yourself stumbling over stringing more than two sentences together to engage yourself intelligently in conversation.

But all you really need to know is approximately 100 phrases and you'll be able to string sentence after sentence with ease. In contrast you'll be surprised how much more fluent you'll be. If you know 1,000 separate words, you may be able to correctly create one sentence. Only one sentence.

If you learn 100 phrases you'll be able to speak many more sentences. And if you get ambitious and learn 1,000 phrases (it's not nearly as difficult as it seems) . . . well . . . you'll be nearly as fluent as a native speaker.

Once you learn even a few of these phrases a week, your understanding of speaking this language with explode exponentially. The trick is to learn the phrase so well that you only have to exert a small amount effort on completing them.

Listed below are several of the most common phrases in the language. How many of them do you know? If you find there are some you're stumbling over, then you may want to study those some.

- *How often do you (plus verb)?*
- *Can I help you (plus verb or as a question by itself)?*
- *It's too late for that*
- *You could have (plus a verb)*
- *If I were you I would have (add verb)*
- *It looks like (plus a noun)*
- *It's time to (plus a verb)*
- *What if (plus a subject and verb)*
- *How was (plus a noun)*
- *Let's say that (plus subject and verb)*
- *I think I should (plus a verb)*
- *I'm sorry to (plus a verb)*
- *I was thinking about (plus a verb)*
- *I think I should (plus a verb)*
- *Thank you for (plus a verb)*

- *I don't know what to do about (plus a noun)*

- *Have you ever thought about (plus a verb)?*

Using just one of those phrases, you're about to see how many different situations it's suited for:

Have you ever thought about (plus a verb)?

- Have you ever thought about starting your business?
- Have you ever thought about changing jobs?
- Have you ever thought about learning how to swim?
- Have you ever thought about becoming a writer?
- Have you ever thought about having more children?
- Have you ever thought about selling your house?
- Have you ever thought about visiting South America?
- Have you ever thought about learning Russian?
- Have you ever thought about the meaning of life?
- Have you ever thought about joining a fitness center?

If you learned just this one phrase, you can immediately see how many ways you can use it in daily conversation. This phrase, in particular, is a great example, because when you ask it, you're inviting someone into a conversation with you. That will spawn the use of even more sentences using phrases you've already learned.

Can you see how pointless it becomes to learn individual words when your ultimate aim is to speak more fluently? That's not to say that learning more words isn't important. But don't forget to give a priority to learning phrases as well.

3. Think in English

When you go to speak to someone, don't think in your native language and then translate your sentence into English. Simply think in English. This is one of those guidelines that is easier said than done. You're trying to break a habit – thinking in your native tongue – that has been with you all of your life. To be honest, you probably don't know any other way to think.

Why is thinking in your native language not a particularly good idea? The ordering of the words in your native language is more than language not going to be the same as in the English language. Your natural tendency will be to repeat the English words in that order.

But more than that, in the process of translating your sentence, you'll probably be trying to use grammar rules you're not all that familiar with yet.

Thinking in English will, undoubtedly be difficult at first, but the more you force your mind to do it, easier it becomes. And the easier it becomes, the more fluent you'll be at the English language. Give it a try the next time you go to speak English.

4. Practice speaking English when you hear it.

Remember that reading and listening to the English word doesn't make you a better speaker. It will give you more knowledge of reading the written word and understanding it when it is spoken to you. But learning to speak it yourself, requires you do more work. It requires that you truly become interactive with the language.

Without a doubt, reading and listening to the language are two of the most important aspects of learning English. But you're missing the final piece of the puzzle if you don't practice speaking it. This goes for any language, not just English.

Think about the order in which young children learn their native language. They first learn how to speak it and become quite fluent in it and finally learn how to read. Yes, I know that in the process they make many grammatical mistakes. One of the most common is to use the word "brung" as a past tense form of "bring." The correct form is brought. "Look what I've brung you." But the vital point is they didn't wait until they knew what the proper form of the verb was before they spoke. And they do indeed get their message across.

So, don't obsess with reading and listening. It appears the natural order of learning a language is listening, speaking, reading and then writing. So don't think for a moment that your reading and writing skills aren't good enough to allow you to speak it. Your average four-year-old doesn't seem to worry about it.

5. Surround yourself with others who speak English

I've said it before and I'll say it again: immerse yourself in the English language. Compare the English language to an ocean. As long as you stay on the ship you'll only learn what's at the surface of the ocean. Sure, you'll have a great view of the waves and you know the temperature by dipping your hands in the water occasionally. But you'll never know what lies beneath the surface unless you immerse yourself – submerge yourself – into the body of water.

If you don't the plunge from the boat into the ocean right now, when will you?

Think about this for a moment. Those English students who excel at speaking the language are usually the individuals who attended – or are still attending – an English-speaking school. Why is that? Because they were in a culture that forced them to speak English. If they had their way they might have preferred to speak more in their own language.

But they took all their classroom lessons in English, talked to their professors in English – even talked to their friends in English.

Compare these individuals to those who studied abroad, but returned lamenting they still aren't fluent in the language. Because all the while they were in an English-speaking country they never allowed themselves to take the plunge. For whatever reason, they never took the plunge into fully using what skills they had developed up to that time?

So does that mean you have to travel or go to an English-speaking school in order to speak the language fluently? No, not by a long shot. You can become fluent in the language without ever traveling anywhere! Simply make a pact with your friends who are also learning the language that you're all going to dive into the ocean of English to learn what's beneath the surface.

Promise each other then when gathered you'll only speak English. Don't have that many friends who are English speakers or learning the language? Before you know it you'll find yourself thinking in English when you're around these individuals and speaking in the language won't seem so frightening any longer.

Made in the USA
San Bernardino, CA
12 July 2018